GRANDPA'S CHAIR

BY: DEBBY FEO

ILLUSTRATED
BY:____

Dedicated to: my husband John (who enables me to write); my kids: Teresa and Mike (who were my inspiration); my sisters: Kathy, Jody, and Carol (the subjects); my "big brother" Joe (who always encouraged); and mustn't forget Grandpa and Grandma Selker; Aunt Noni (Naomi) Herman; and Uncle Leon Herman. Special Thanks to my mother, Barbara (Selker) Motter, who is now one of Heaven's Librarians.

Order this book online at www.trafford.com/08-0542
or email orders@trafford.com

Most Trafford titles are also available at major online book retailers.

Cover Design/Artwork by Teresa Feo

Note for Librarians: A cataloguing record for this book is available from Library and Archives Canada at www.collectionscanada.ca/amicus/index-e.html

ISBN: 978-1-4251-7705-8

www.trafford.com

North America & international
toll-free: 1 888 232 4444 (USA & Canada)
phone: 250 383 6864 • fax: 250 383 6804 • email: info@trafford.com

The United Kingdom & Europe
phone: +44 (0)1865 722 113 • local rate: 0845 230 9601
facsimile: +44 (0)1865 722 868 • email: info.uk@trafford.com

10 9 8 7 6 5 4 3 2 1

AUNT NONI

Aunt Noni was a lot of fun
Much loved by all us kids
She'd join us in the breakfast nook
And giggle like we did

Instead of being with adults,
Not much fun to talk to
She'd rather come and sit with us,
Than in the place she ought to

She'd look away, and then look back
And often wouldn't "see"
The pile of veggies on her plate,
Just before was empty

After dinner, with dishes done
Was time for "friendly"cards
Our Aunt believed that she could win
But found it very hard

Once in a while, we'd have some fun
Trying to set her up
We'd pass to her the worst of cards
Until she'd had enough

"Gertie Graball is what you are,
You know I needed that.
Can't you give me something better?
Don't be a dirty rat!"

We knew she didn't mean it mean
The fun was in the play
Whether or not you won or lost
She made a holiday

BAT WARS

The bat, he was just having fun
Flying to and fro
But Grandma did not like the bat
The bat, he had to go

And so began the battle
The bat and Grandma's broom
Grandma did not want the bat
To fly around her room

The bat soared up, the bat swooped down
The broom swung here and there
They made an awful racket
Insults filled the air

Grandpa then came roaring in
"What in the world is wrong?
That little bat won't hurt you."
But he covered his head with his arm

He ran and threw the windows wide
And unclosed both the doors
The bat rushed out into the night
He would return no more

THE BEAR

"Don't go in there" said Grandpa
"There is a bear in there!"
We stayed out of that closet
For fear of that old bear

The years went by and then
I decided to
See that mean, old bear
See what he would do

I gathered up my courage
And slowly climbed the stairs
Walked quietly down the hall
Turned the corner, and was there

Would that old bear eat me?
He must be really starved
Living in the closet
Instead of in the yard

I opened up the door
Carefully, I was prepared
To run away so quickly
If that bear was really there

So dark, I could see little
So I reached up for the string
No bear was in the closet
It was full of wondrous things

Boxes full of treasures
Glassware on the shelves
Discarded childhood toys
Fragile Christmas bells

All my Grandma's memories
Had long been stored up there
Safe from little fingers
Guarded by that bear

THE BIG PINK BED

After bingo, I got to stay
In Noni's big pink bed
Warm soft blankets, so fast asleep
When pillow met my head

Woke up early, in the morning
To lots of tiny smiles
From dolls lined up around the room
With teeth – old fashioned styles

Besides the dolls, were many books
Lined up in their rows
A dream world, still, since hours spent
With book in front of nose

THE BINGO ELVES

They had a job to do
Three little Bingo Elves
Their job to do was one –
Make sure Aunt Noni won

They traveled very far
Aunt Noni's little elves
A long way on the bus
To bring her best of luck

There, she would line them up
Those little Bingo Elves
Over the rows of cards
Stretching out for yards

As the night wore on
Elves got splattered with ink
Her hand came crashing down
Her face was one big frown

Three little Bingo Elves
Had done their very best
As far as I could see
It wasn't meant to be

THE BIRTHDAY SUIT

I never got to live it down
That silly little picture
Me, in the suit mom had made
That caused me grief, for sure

She wrote on back, to my dismay
"Debby - in her birthday suit"
And when my sisters saw it
Then they all began to hoot

Soon, all over the neighborhood
That darn picture made the rounds
As they laughed, I wanted to
Sink right into the ground

My aunt and my uncle got it
But my mother never did
If ***I*** get my hands on it
Those words will get redid

THE BUTTER INCIDENT

The victim was a stick
A stick of yellow butter
It lay upon the floor
Squashed by the foot of my mother

The scene was in the closet
Next to the living room
My mother had gone in
To get and to use her vacuum

Some cleaning was her goal
She didn't turn on the light
Stepped on something squishy
Which gave her a bit of a fright

She switched the light on fast
Then she looked down at her foot
Was shocked to see some butter
Then real trouble was afoot

The girls were called inside
And were lined up in a row
"Who left this butter here?"
Angry mother then wanted to know

The answer soon became
Obvious to all now there
The youngest of them all
Had butter smushed everywhere

CAN I HAVE A PUPPY, PLEASE?

Can you get me a puppy, please?
A "Lassie" dog to keep?
I promise that I'll walk her
And in my bed she'll sleep

She will not be any bother
She won't take up much space
I'll give her some of my food
My veggies won't go to waste

I'll collect a bunch of bottles
And trade them in for dimes
You won't have to do anything
I've got a lot of time

<u>THE CAR AND MR. CLEAN</u>

We had a little blue car
Pedals made it go
It wasn't good for races
The wheels turned much too slow

Only one could ride it
It only had one seat
You couldn't be too big or
You couldn't fit your feet

While my mom washed clothes
The little car, I'd wash
Use the bottle with the bald man
But, water I would slosh

When the car was sparkling clean
My mother dried off me
The car, it dried itself off
And shined for all to see

COMFORT FOOD

Certain foods with special ties
Were cherished by us four girls:
Soft ice cream in a cone
That ended up in swirls

Chili made, *without* the beans
Grandma's potato salad
Sauerkraut with hot dogs
Warm banana nut bread

Fancy little sandwiches
Especially by our aunt
Eating fresh rhubarb stalks
Never purple eggplant!

Real banana popsicles
Been brought as a special treat
Coke in green glass bottles
That tasted oh so sweet

Some s'mores made by the campfire
Jersey corn cooked on the cob
Baked beans from the thermos
Cookie dough by the blob

Peanut butter spread on toast
Or sometimes just plain butter
Turkey on Thanksgiving
Taco Pie by mother

Wise Potato Chips – 10¢
Popcorn all covered with cheese
Marshmallows in cocoa
Fruit from our apple trees

So many tastes remembered
And eaten now when sad
Bring back special memories
Of happy times we had

<u>CRICKET LULLABY</u>

I like to sleep outside at night
And listen to the crickets
Some people do not like it
As they make a lot of racket

Crickets can help me fall asleep
When my head's too full of scenes
When I've got too many plans
Or, for the next day I'm too keen

DADDY LONGLEGS

I don't know why they call them daddy
But, they certainly have long legs
You could find them in my cellar
Sitting calmly in their webs

Mother would tell me not to worry
Because, they weren't the biting ones
In fact, they were very helpful
Eating bad bugs by the tons

I really tried hard to believe her
But sometimes, couldn't help but jump
Especially if, I ran into
A spider webby clump

ELEPHANT TUG

The big, gray elephant
And my sister and me
Were having a battle
For all to see

He was winning the war
He didn't seem to mind
The rope that was tied
To his behind

His goal was the cart
The cart with the loot
Big, green melons
His favorite fruit

I don't think he felt
Big sister and me
He didn't even know
That he wasn't free

FAMILY PHOTOS

Aunt Noni was the keeper
Of albums filled with lore
With pictures of people who
We'd never seen before

That's your uncle as a boy
Here's one of your mother
This one with the frowning face
Is of my father's brother

There's Leon in the Army
So many years ago
And this is me and Leon
While playing in the snow

Most of them were black and white
Some were funny yellow
Some of them looked colored in
By children long ago

Held tight by little corners
On pages, blackest black
Tied together by a string
And kept all in a stack

THE FIRE TOWER

Up and up and up we went
"Grandpa, how much higher?"
We climbed and climbed
Forever, it seemed
Up that fire tower

"Please stay away from the edge
Remember, do not run!"
We slowed our feet
But were bound to look –
Looking's half the fun

Near the top, we had to stop
We'd search the trees all 'round
Scanning for smoke
No one else could see,
A fire not yet found

We felt like Smokey's helpers
With carelessness our foe
Great gusts of wind
Would shake the tower
Whip our hair and clothes

Going down was not as fun
But downwards we were pulled
More trails to hike
Cool creeks to wade, and
Grandpa's hand to hold

FOUR HORNED BUGS

You know those nasty
Four "horned" bugs?
That sometimes come out
From shoes and rugs?

I do not really
Like those things
If one gets near me
Away I'll spring

With horns up front
Pinchers behind
I can like most bugs
But not ***that*** kind

FRECKLES

I always wanted a collie
"Lassie" would be her name
But Freckles came into our life
Not looking quite the same

With little spots upon her nose
Shaved off little tummy
With ears that stood at attention
Not long gone from mommy

"Cookie" dog treats were her passion
Kitties were for chasing
Chewing up whatever she saw
Trails were meant for racing

Around the house, both up and down
All inside and then out
Suddenly, she'd run out of steam
And plop down right about

Where every person had to walk
The middle of the action
The slightest move would wake her up
So instant her reaction

The cats were glad when she went out
They'd run to feed and drink
Quickly getting business done
Then hiding in a blink

FRIENDLY TREES

My sister said
She talked to "Susan"
Who was I to disbelieve?
But the big, blue pine
At the end of the field
Never talked to me

Our Uncle Leon
Would make us houses
Under the "Christmas" trees
He would chop off all
The lowest branches
Which gave us room to be

Sometimes we would climb
Way up those pines
To get a better view
Our hands and arms
Would get black and grimy
From the sticky pine tree goo

THE G. C. MURPHY HORSES

Whenever I got some change
For a pop bottle or two
I'd set off on a mission
Many blocks, I would walk to

The big old "Five and Ten Store"
Had lots of things to buy
But I always chose the same
Why because? I'll tell you why

There were many plastic horses
Of many different hues
My goal was, to get for me
As many as I could choose

They didn't need a rider
After all, they were quite wild
They just needed some new friends
They needed to be stockpiled

Sometimes the pretty black one
Would get to be "Horse King"
Then later, the pure white one
Would have the run of things

Scarlet horse had a temper
To go along with his fur
He'd run so fast right by you
He looked just like a blur

Special was the old, tan horse
Who always had a hurt foot
Someone, among my sisters
Had bitten off, his left hoof

<u>GLO BUGS</u>

After the sun set on summer nights
We would still run around, without fright

As we played a lot of silly games
Many made up ones, and ones with names

As soon as we got too tired of those
We'd run around, with grass in our toes

When we decided we couldn't see
We'd look for glo-bugs, near the tree

With holes punched out of an old jar lid
We'd catch those bugs, wherever they hid

Little lightening bugs caught in jars
Would then become, our own private stars

GRANDPA

His hair was white, his belly large
His eyes were sparkling blue
If you were bored, you went to him
For something fun to do

His head was full of stories
About the days gone by
Of trips down south to Florida
Or of Grandma, who would sigh

"It didn't happen that way at all!"
"But that's the way it was!"
He'd wink at us and then would say,
"I remember more than she does."

GRANDPA'S CHAIR

You could fly to the moon
In Grandpa's chair
Or zoom to a faraway planet
The only problem with that chair
Was to find it
Without Grandpa on it

Quick, it's empty
Now's the chance
Dash into the room
Fight for the right
To be the pilot
Quick, he'll be back soon

Turn the switch
Higher, higher
Blast into the stars
Off to explore
Strange new worlds
Flying, oh so far

GRASSHOPPER SCHOOL

When summer came and we were bored
We'd go into the field
And catch a bunch of grasshoppers
And set them up in school

We'd teach those unlearned bugs
How to jump real high
Over sticks and over twigs
By pushing their behinds

Our fingers got so very brown
From spitting hopper-juice
We liked to watch them chewing sideways
Food – the grassy kinds

After they had learned to jump
Back to the field they went
We couldn't keep them in a jar
Our mom said that was cruel

HALLOWEEN WALK

We got to go wherever we wanted
As long as we could walk
Our rules were: home for meals,
And be back before dark

The longest walks we ever took
Occurred on Halloween
We'd dress up in our costumes
And join the Marching Teams

We met in front of "Garby's"
And got all in a line
Bands, and cars, and fire trucks
And tried to march in time

All the parents stood along
The route that we would march
Waving, yelling, taking pictures
As we strutted to the park

The dressed-up kids kept going
To the fire house garage
Were given lots of candy and
Warnings too, because

All the kids, on their way home
Would stop at all the houses
That had a light upon their porch
To contribute to our causes

Gathering bags of candy
To eat for many days
Hopefully not, to make us sick
Or cause us tooth decay

<u>THE HAMSTER MONSTER</u>

"J" didn't say a word
Hoping for no notice
Couldn't just look at it
She just *had* to hold it

The brand new pet escaped
Wiggled out of her hand
There was no sign of it
It wasn't close at hand

Where had the hamster gone?
It wasn't on the floor
It ran up my mother's leg
Very hard to ignore

"Aagh!" she screamed in panic
"What's crawling up my leg?"
The hamster ran and hid
My mother's face burned red

No one dared make a sound
My mother stopped the car
Caught the troublemaker
A *monster* pet so far

HERMAN'S STORE

Herman's store was a wonderful place
Was then, and still is
Kids and grownups would stop by
Just to shoot the breeze

Our Uncle Leon was the magnet
Pulling people there
If you needed a kindly ear
He had one to spare

To some he was known as "Hermie"
A "must-see" every day
Students would drop in for candy
Start talking, then would stay

Oh, the things that you could buy
If you had a dime
Even with just a nickel
Choosing would take time

"How about a couple of these?"
Red, black licorice
Everything for a penny
All that you could wish

Finally, with our choices made
We'd clutch our little sacks
Rush next door, or go on home
And have a little snack

We were the envy of other kids
He was ***our*** Uncle Leon
We agreed that we were lucky
We knew it even then

THE HUNT

Grandpa led the way
For the band of happy hikers
Spread out in a line
The brave, wild beastie likers

"Hope we see a lion
Maybe spot some deer!"
"Only if you're quiet
They will not let you near."

"What's that over there?
A bear, it is a bear!"
"No," said our wise Grandpa
"Only a bush, my dear."

"No one make a sound
Quietly we must go
Something's moving over there
Look, it is a doe!"

Shortly, it was time to turn
And head back to the cabin
Little legs were all worn out
Tummies were a grumblin'

Almost home, almost there
Talk of roasting hot dogs
Grandpa didn't notice
The littlest stop by a log

"Here kitty, kitty!" filled the air
"What?" said Grandpa stopping
He turned around and wailed "Oh No!"
And soon he was a hopping

He sprinted back, grabbed her up
Then hurried back to us
“Skunk!” he yelled, “Run!” he screamed
We ran without a fuss

We ran uphill and downhill twice
Until we reached the cabin
We dashed inside to spread the news
Then ran right out again

“That was fun, let’s walk some more
Let’s go and find that skunk!”
“Oh no, no way”, sighed Grandpa
“it’s time to have some lunch.”

I'LL NEVER TELL!

Hanging over the stair's side
Not in bed when I was sick
I watched TV upside down
I thought it was a great trick

Fell off the too-big bike
In front of the hospital
Had to limp the whole way home
But of course I would not tell

Suzanne's chasing me around
Got me trouble at the school
Running inside the classroom
Breaking an important rule

Sister "losing" her snow pants
"Someone took them by mistake"
Really she had buried them
In a bank, made of snowflakes

"Breaking" sounds would make us hide
Everyone would disappear
We never knew who'd done it
Because none of us were near

While out on Elsie's horse farm
Her cow stepping on my toe
Just one more thing kept inside
My mother would never know

JUDY, WHERE ARE YOU?

"Judy, Judy, Judy"
Said the man with the mike
"Judy, Judy, Judy…
Come and get your bike!"

But Jody, Jody, Jody
Didn't really think
Jody, Jody, Jody
Was what he really meant

But Jane saw the problem
So she jumped up to say
"Here she is, here's Jody!"
That's how Jane saved the day

Jody, Jody, Jody
Got a brand new bike
Saturday at the movies
From the man with the mike

KANGAROO HOP

Two kangaroos
Hopped all around the room
Each had a pouch. with a baby

Two small kangaroos
Just as cute as could be
My sister, Kathy, and me

With brown and white tummies
Our ears striped black
We peeked out of eyeholes, so tiny

Sticking out from behind
Were two long tails
That swished back and forth, quite nicely

With little brown paw-hands
Fantastic fur
And perfect for jumping, big feet

We were dressed to go out
On Halloween night
Courtesy of, Aunt Noni

LESSONS

Give Grandpa a stream
You'd have hours of fun
Wading, or fishing with sticks

Push over a stone
Catch a crayfish
Behind the claws is the trick

"That flat stone is good,
Throw under like this."
To skip across the stream

"Those *fish* are tadpoles,
They'll turn into frogs."
Grab and jar and float some in

"What about our shoes?
They are getting wet?"
"Go ahead and take them off."

"Watch out for your socks,
If they float away,
Then your Grandma will get hot!"

After time flew by
All muddy and wet
Back to the cabin we'd tread

Grandma would meet us
By the door and sigh
Scold Grandpa, and shake her head

LITTLE BROWN COOKIES

Oh, they *really* were awful
Those little, brown cookies she made
Although she'd been so proud of them
On the plate, most of them stayed

One little thing she forgot
Of the ingredients she took
Remembered the root beer flavor
Sugar, she forgot to put

Happily, she brought them in
She wanted ev'ryone to try
Everyone then made a face
She almost started to cry

LITTLE CABIN

Little cabin, number one
Set beside a stream
Site of many happy days
In the rain or sun-beam

Every year we'd go up there
To the little cabin
The highlight of the summer
Was being there again

Grandma would do the cooking
Grandpa did the fun
We'd follow him around the woods
Until the day was done

When it got too dark to see
Grandpa called us in
To tell us a good story
Of somewhere that he'd been

We'd toss off dirty clothes
Dress in warm pajamas
Then climb up wooden ladders
To get some sleep because

Grandpa had more adventures
Planned for the next day
If we didn't get our rest
We'd be too tired to play

LITTLE GREEN HOUSE

The little, green house
Was special to us
It had lots of special things. . .

Like a stepstool in the kitchen
On which to watch Grandma cook
A drawer in the dining room
Filled with toys and coloring books

A closet we never went in
The one Grandpa said had a bear
A fancy, mirrored place to sit
To "put on your face" and brush hair

Grandpa's chair in the living room
That was our spaceship to the stars
And a great, big, many-roomed basement
Filled with boxes and canning jars

A bedroom where all was purple
To sleep in when on a visit
A breakfast nook, sunny yellow
Where the kids and Noni would sit

And best of all
Not least of all
Grandma and Grandpa S.

LONGFELLOW TRAIL

It was the trail
The longest trail
The longest and the toughest
Only when you were big enough
Did Grandpa take you on it

Too many hills
Too many streams
Wild animals galore
Couldn't have legs that got worn out
You had to be at least four

Before the hike
Grandpa would talk
To the ones he'd pull aside
Too little to, be able to
Keep up, although they tried

"Next year, maybe"
Grandpa would say
"Bet you'll grow about double
Just for now," he'd wink and say
"Keep Grandma out of trouble!"

"We'll be back soon,
Then later on,
We'll take our own little hike.
Just you and me, to dig for worms,
The juicy ones, that fish like."

MOMMY, I LOVE YOU!

She always got there first
Don't really know just why
After kicking my shin
Then away she would fly

Before I'd get inside
To tattle tale on her
She'd be hugging my mom
And sweetly telling her

"Mommy, mommy - love you
I really, really do!"
When I'd come limping in
The next minute or two

Too late I was again
Who would ever believe
That such a small, cute girl
Ever tried to deceive

MONSTER FURNACE

Round and round
And around we went
All around the furnace
Racing, racing, oh so fast
On our little trikes

Sometimes, that big, old furnace
Would let out frightening sounds
Off the trikes
And up we'd run
To safety and our mother

There were some rooms
In that cellar
We didn't dare go into
Who knew what creatures lurked in there
Friends of the monster furnace

NOT ALWAYS GOOD

The youngest of our sisters got
Much attention from our parents
But she also had to put up with
Teasing, as a consequence

"If you swallow watermelon seeds
They'll grow inside your tummy."
"You can have all my brussel sprouts,
Go ahead, they're really yummy!"

Our clothes were handed down so much
They were all stretched out at the waist
Only the oldest sister might ever get
Clothes to suit her taste

But one good thing, for the youngest
Was the relaxing of the rules
She wasn't forced, like the rest of us
To wear snowpants to our school

NOT GOING AWAY!

"He's both'ring me!"
She told her mom
When he wouldn't go away

"He cries and wets
And smells real bad!"
Made it hard for her to play

"Can't he go back?"
She asked her mom
But brother was there to stay

OH NO! A DRAGON!

We stopped on the way to the condo
Of Grandpa and Grandma S.
On the long drive down to Florida
To visit one of my aunts

We stayed for a couple of days
The kids, on the screened-in porch
We slept in colorful sleeping bags
That we had to roll up, of course

Returning one morning to do this
A tiny, green "dragon" I found
I rolled up the bag, very quickly
Without making a sound

My mother didn't understand
I became a bit of a grouch
I refused to sleep in my bag
Would only sleep on the couch

Next day, I started to worry
That the dragon couldn't breathe
I quickly threw open the bag
No dragon – what a relief!

THE OWEY

"I've got an owey, Mommy!
Right here on the top
It hurts real bad
See, Mommy
Won't you make it stop?"

Mommy stopped and took a look,
Then put down the dish
Cleaned the hurt and
Bandaged it,
Healed it with a kiss

POODLES, COLLIES, AND MUTTS

I couldn't really have a dog
So I had to just make do
I had a lot of small, stuffed dogs
Of purple, green and blue

I made them leashes out of string
And around the yard I'd drag
They would bounce along behind me
Until their heads would sag

I'd brush their fur every day
So they wouldn't get too worn
Clean them up with Ivory soap
And bandage up the torn

The most beloved of all my dogs
Was the collie that could "sing"
She always went along with me
The best of anything

PRAYING FOR BUGS

They were the longest bugs I knew
The great, big praying mantis
I'd find them in the vacant lot
Walking slow, I would not miss

Their light green color was pleasing
And the fact that they were calm
At times I even got a bug
To sit quietly on my palm

They seemed to look right back at me
With a haughty little stare
Wondering why I bothered them
While they were saying their prayer

THE QUEEN FLIES

When the littlest of the sisters
Sometimes would get left out
She'd have to play her own games
Like flying, here and about

She'd put on her flying robe
Really, her much loved blanket
She'd jump off from "high" places
And fly around the carpet

With the flying, came a song
"Oh, ***I*** am the flying queen!"
Superwoman in disguise
Her favorite have-fun scene

RELATIVES AND FRIENDS

Noni had a lot of friends
Many relatives galore
Horsey, Elsie MacGregor
And the founders – Herman's Store

Papa Paul was her father
Uncle Lorry played violin
"Big Joe" wasn't quite all there
Father Joe was next of kin

She talked of Grandma Lizzy
Of Ireland far away
Stories of how people came
To America to stay

How they all came to settle
In villages all around
Starting up their families
Setting up a brand new town

SHAKING PAWS

When “Lassie” was on
I’d rush to the room
Adventures in black and white
In every show
Something would go wrong
Giving Timmy a bit of a fright

But Lassie always
Would save the day, she
Always took care of her boy
So the little dog
That looked just like her
Became my favorite toy

At the end of the show
During the credits
Lassie would raise her paw
There would be a fight
Of anyone there
Who’d get to shake, what they saw

THE SLEDDING HILL

With our best friends, Jane and Elaine
We'd go to the "hospital hill"
Pulling our little wooden sleds
I fondly remember it still

After jumping onto the sleds
We would push ourselves with our feet
Go flying off down the steep hill
Swerving to avoid spots of sleet

We'd start out to the right, not left
In hopes of avoiding the tree
Near the bottom, stick out our feet
Then tumble off our sleds with glee

We kept trudging back, up the hill
That was harder up than down
Pulling behind our frozen sleds
With our snow hats an icy crown

Eventually, we would quit
When our little toes got too cold
It was surely time to go home
When your hands could no longer hold

SNOWCAVE

He built for us
One wintry day
A cave of snow
To hide away

He squished inside
But was too big
The snow cave fell
So out we dig

Covered with snow
Laughing with glee
Wonderful day
Wonderful deed

SPECIAL DISHES

Special dishes red or green,
Or with roses on their sides
Would appear on holidays
From the places they would hide

On Christmas or on New Year's
Thanksgiving and Easter too
The family gathered 'round
The tables, one and two

Little kids with itchy feet
Had a table all their own
So grownups could just sit and talk
Not listen to them moan

Kids would run around and play
As the grownups would catch up
On all the latest gossip
Drinking coffee from their cups

All the women took their time
They were not in a hurry to
Tackle dirty dishes
Or the pots they had to do

SUNDAYS AT AUNT NONI'S

Almost like a tradition
Sunday afternoons with Noni
After lunch, we'd walk up there
To watch a musical movie

Sometimes, we would get lucky
And would get to stay for supper
Cold sandwiches by our aunt
Pop from the store, like Dr. Pepper

Next, Uncle Leon would bring
For dessert, vanilla ice cream
Eaten out of special bowls
At the end, we'd lick them clean

Leon made funny faces
Aunt Noni loudly smacked her lips
These two, they caused much laughter
With their funny little quips

TICK TOCK

Tick and tock and tick and tock
From Grandma R's little clock
Rolled around inside my head
As I lay in her guest bed

Light snuck in under the door
Old house smell, along the floor
Mothballs and the scent of bleach
Polish on the wood antiques

Voices heard from down below
First were high and then went low
Quilts kept off the snowy cold
As done for years, very old

All alone, not used to it
Great big bed and one small kid
Special night and special treat
Finally, drift off to sleep

TREES IN SPACE

We had two spaceship trees
Out back behind our house
Two little apple trees
That took us all about

We'd load up on supplies
With dolls as passengers
Then flying side by side
We'd take off with a grrrr!

The apples weren't so good
In fact were very sour
But gave us good defense,
Made the "bad guys" cower

We'd stay up in those trees
Till hunger brought us down
Friends came by to visit
Or bedtime rolled around

THE TRICKY BEAR

Little Brown Bear rolled under the fence
Big smile upon his face
He went to the people watching
And begged them for a snack

"Don't feed the bears!" the Ranger had warned
"It is not good for them!
It's much better for little bears
To only learn Bear ways."

Little Brown Bear, seeing the Ranger
Rolled back under the fence
He acted like he was busy
Just playing with his toys

The Ranger left, again Little Bear
Rolled back out where he'd been
Put his paws out for some food and
Everybody laughed

UNCLE LEON

Walking was his passion
To river's edge and back
Searching for old bottles
Mementos from the past

He'd dig for flasks and vials
Then wash them out and look
Clues to age and purpose
With help of antique books

The glass would be displayed
On shelves around his store
Sparkling in the sunshine
With scarcely room for more

Though paths have changed with time
He's on the lookout still
Seeker of lost bottles
With stories as their fill

VERY BEARLY THERE

My mom told me a story
That came from her childhood
Of a time that she went camping
At a cabin in the wood

She woke up very late at night
Thinking she had heard a sound
She looked out of a window
And there, a bear, she found

She couldn't believe her eyes
And neither could the bear
Neither knew just what to do
So kept on standing there

Suddenly, my mother screamed
Which really scared the bear
Both turned around and ran away
To be anywhere, but there

WARMED AND DRIED

The cold, wet worms were drowning
In all that mushy mud
Sister came to the rescue
The rest of us said, "Ugh!"

She pulled out the worms with care
And put them on a ledge
"Dry out you poor, little worms
I'll be back soon, " she pledged

Afterwards she ran to play
The time went zooming by
The worms turned into twigs and
Sister began to cry

WHEN JODY WAS LEFT BEHIND

My mother'd rather not remember
That time we stopped at the farm
On our yearly summer vacation trip
Since Jody never came to harm

My sister didn't even notice
That she'd even been left behind
She was playing with all the kittens
Was having a really good time

We were on a trip to Florida
And had stopped at a friendly farm
To stretch our legs and eat some food
And soak up some country charm

After eating lunch and packing up
We all piled back into the car
Was Mother's turn to be the driver
But we didn't get very far

A puzzled look came over her face
Was there something she'd forgotten?
Glanced back at us, as if for a clue
As if something there was rotten

All of a sudden she turned the car
And squealed her way back to the farm
Ran to the barn to get my sister
Laughing, not even alarmed

WHERE HAVE ALL THE DRIVE-INS GONE?

There seem to be a few still left
But most of them are now done
Those wonderful drive-in movies
Where we kids had lots of fun

Piled into the family car
With our blankets and a pillow
Went early for the best spots and
A speaker not too low

Puffed Cheese and "made-at-home" popcorn
And red Kool-Aid from our mom
But by the time we got there,
Sleep had overtaken some

WHO'S AFRAID?

"I'm not afraid of bears.
I'm telling you, it's true.
Just don't get in their way,
And they won't bother you."

They parked up on the road
And hiked down to the river
Grandma set up chairs
With Grandpa fishing near her

"Oh, no a bear is there!
Do pay attention please.
Don't you see it coming?
I think that we should leave!"

"We are not bothering him.
It's not a problem, dear."
"I don't care," said Grandma
"I am not staying here!"

Grandpa stayed there fishing
Grandma started for home
Grandma didn't mention
That the bear was not alone

The bear was with her cubs
She didn't want to share
Any fish with Grandpa
Or even want him near

Grandpa soon joined Grandma
He sat down with a sigh
"Okay, I'm done, let's go home."
He wouldn't say just why

Later on that day
When Grandma washed his shirt
While checking in his pocket
She found a mound of dirt

As an added bonus
Now crawling up her arm
Leaving squiggly trails
Were Grandpa's fishing worms

She ran up from the cellar
While shaking off her wrist
Then she asked of Grandpa
"Would you mind explaining this?"

THE XMAS CATALOGUE

One of the most important things
Would happen without fail
The Sear's Christmas catalogue
Would come to us in the mail

My mother had us circle
In different colored ink
What we wanted for Christmas
As many as we could think

We rarely, if ever, would
Get anything we circled
But the fun was in the hope
That still Santa would be told

X RAY VISION – NO□!

I couldn't see
My glasses broke
But to Grandma's
I must go

An errant ball
Had hit my nose
Down the middle
They had cracked

I knew the way
But objects loomed
With hazy
Unclear edges

Distances seemed
Were all gone wrong
But finally
I got there

Familiar sights
The Grandma voice
Seemed to be so
Different

A strange new world
Was ruled so by
My weakly, poor
Seeing eyes

YOU CAN'T FOOL A HORSE

The big, red horse, I'm sure he knew
That I didn't know what to do

Some instructions had been given
But the horse was not forgiving

First, he headed towards a tree
Hoping branches, I didn't see

As I managed to stay on board
The horse glanced at me, with a snort

Plotting the next thing he would do
Then the ocean came into his view

Brown eyes gleamed, he headed for shore
Started twisting, and I was sure

He meant to roll, over on me
So that of me, he would be free

Off I jumped and then off he went
Back to the barn and fresh hay scent

ZOOMING DOWN THE STREET

I was really angry
Decided to run away
Made some peanut butter toast
To eat along the way

I got upon my trike
And I headed up the block
Passed by my neighbors' houses and
Even the vacant lot

I pedaled really fast
As fast as my legs would go
Made it to the alley, then
Stopped to look to and fro

That's where my mom caught up
She was angrier than me
'Cause she was really worried
Since I was only three

PAJAMAZ WITH FEET

"Red Rover, Red Rover"
Play over and over
Sing and dance off to Oz
Why because? Just because!

Dodge ball and softball
And kickball and volleyball
Teach grasshoppers some school
Put frogs in the swim pool

Wagons and tricycles
Pedal car, bicycles
Roller skates stuck on shoes
Jacks – way far past the "Two's"

Many scabs on each knee
Climb up the blue, pine tree
Sticky pitch…sticky hand
Watch "Gilligan's Island"

Of course, some trees can talk
Go everywhere – walk
Yes, stuffed dogs can be real
Go home just for a meal

Get sunburns and bug bites
Have sister and friend fights
Breathe in that "new road smell"
Tar on shoes – "Do Not Tell!"

The day is almost gone
Toys all over the lawn
When it's too dark to see
In our house, we "Must Be!"

Put on pj's with feet
Go to porch made for sleep
Crickets chirp thru the night
Bugs glow with their own light

www.ingramcontent.com/pod-product-compliance
Ingram Content Group UK Ltd.
Pitfield, Milton Keynes, MK11 3LW, UK
UKHW051129260726
13967UKWH00010B/2944

9 781425 177058